Read-About® Math

Can You Guess?

By Brian Sargent

Consultant
Linda Bullock
Math Curriculum Specialist

Children's Press®
A Division of Scholastic Inc.
New York   Toronto   London   Auckland   Sydney
Mexico City   New Delhi   Hong Kong
Danbury, Connecticut

Designer: Herman Adler Design
Photo Researcher: Caroline Anderson
The photo on the cover shows a bag of peanuts.

Library of Congress Cataloging-in-Publication Data

Sargent, Brian.
  Can you guess? / by Brian Sargent.
      p. cm. — (Rookie read-about math)
  Includes bibliographical references and index.
  ISBN 0-516-24421-3 (lib. bdg.)   0-516-24669-0 (pbk.)
  1. Estimation theory—Juvenile literature.
  I. Title. II. Series.
  QA276.8.S257 2004
  519.5'44—dc22
                                        2004005021

CHILDREN'S PRESS, and ROOKIE READ-ABOUT®,
and associated logos are trademarks and or registered trademarks
of Scholastic Library Publishing. SCHOLASTIC and associated logos
are trademarks and or registered trademarks of Scholastic Inc.
1 2 3 4 5 6 7 8 9 10 R 13 12 11 10 09 08 07 06 05 04

Let's go to the zoo!

Here are the tigers. How
many tigers do you see?

There are three tigers.

Let's go see the elephants.
How many elephants do
you see?

There are four elephants.

Let's buy some peanuts to feed the elephants.

Can you guess how many peanuts are in this bag?

10

There are too many to count. When there are too many of something, you have to guess.

We can make a close guess. Divide the peanuts into two equal groups.

1   2

Now count the group
that looks like it has the
most peanuts.

Count the peanuts in
box 1. It looks like it has
the most peanuts.

How many can you count?

1   2

1　　　　　　　**2**

Did you count 14 peanuts in box 1? Since there are two boxes, add the number 14 two times.

$$\begin{array}{r} 14 \\ +\ 14 \\ \hline 28 \end{array}$$

You guessed it. There are 28 peanuts in all!

Let's visit the fish. These fish are called carp.

Can you count how many carp are in the water?

19

There are too many to
count. So, let's guess.

Divide the carp into
four equal groups.

Box 2 has the most carp.
How many carp can
you count?

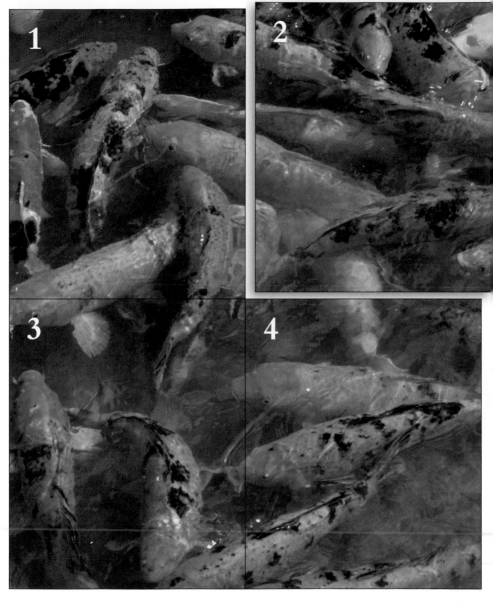

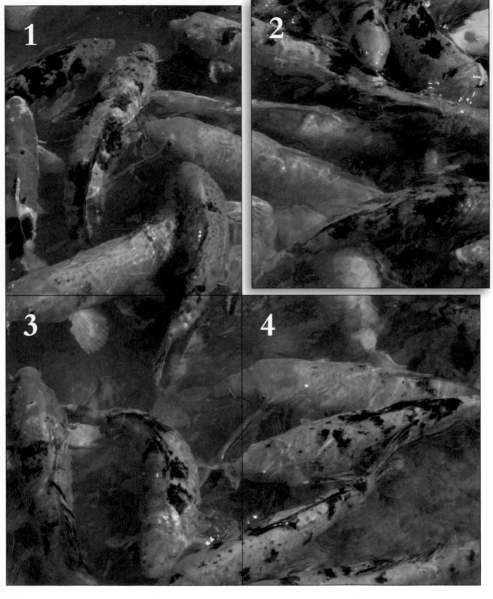

Did you count 10 carp?
Since there are four
boxes, add the number
10 four times.

$$\begin{array}{r} 10 \\ 10 \\ 10 \\ + \ 10 \\ \hline 40 \end{array}$$

You guessed it. There are
40 carp in all!

Sometimes you can guess when you can't see something.

Look at this giraffe. Can you guess how many spots are on both sides of the giraffe's neck?

25

Count the spots in this box.
Did you count 12 spots?

Since there are spots on both sides of the giraffe's neck, add 12 two times.

$$\begin{array}{r} 12 \\ +\ 12 \\ \hline 24 \end{array}$$

You guessed it. There are 24 spots in all!

How many eyespots does
this peacock have?

Can you guess?

eyespots

Words You Know

carp

elephants

giraffe

peacock

peanuts

31

Index

addition, 17, 23, 27

carp, 18, 20, 23

counting, 11, 14, 18, 20, 23, 26

division, 12, 20

eyespots, 28

fish, 18, 20, 23

giraffes, 24, 26–27

groups, 12, 14, 20

guessing, 8, 11–12, 17, 20, 23, 24, 27, 28

peacock, 28

peanuts, 8, 11–12, 14, 17

spots, 24, 26–27

tigers, 4

zoo, 3

About the Author

Brian Sargent is a math teacher in Austin, Texas. He estimates that he has taught for about 5 years.

Photo Credits

Photographs ©2004: Corbis Images: 5 (Bettmann), 7, 30 bottom (Gerald French), 25, 26, 31 top (Danny Lehman), 19, 21, 22, 30 top (George D. Lepp), 3 (Gabe Palmer), 29, 31 bottom left (Chase Swift); Envision Stock Photography Inc./Steven Mark Needham: cover, 9; PictureQuest/Richard Harris//Index Stock Imagery: 10, 13, 15, 16, 31 bottom right.

ML

12/05